The Remarkable Journey of Kayla Harrison

The Inspiring Story of Kayla Harrison, Olympic Judo Champion and How She Conquers Adversity, Achieves Unprecedented Success, and Makes History

Jessica A. Miles

Copyright © 2024 Jessica A. Miles

All rights reserved. No part of this publication may be reproduced, distributed, or transmitted in any form or by any means, including photocopying, recording, or other electronic or mechanical methods, without the prior written permission of the publisher, except in the case of brief quotations embodied in critical reviews and certain other noncommercial uses permitted by copyright law

Table Of Contents

Introduction

Chapter 1

Early Years and Judo Journey

Chapter 2

Olympic Triumphs and World Championships

Chapter 3

Transition to Mixed Martial Arts

Chapter 4

PFL Domination and Rising Stardom

Chapter 5

Signing with Bellator MMA and Return to PFL

Chapter 6

UFC Debut and Beyond

Conclusion

Introduction

Kayla Harrison's journey from a small town to global recognition is a testament to her incredible talent, unwavering determination, and resilience in the face of adversity. Born on July 2, 1990, in Middletown, Ohio, Kayla's early years were marked by a love for sports and an indomitable spirit.

Growing up in a modest household, Kayla was introduced to judo at the tender age of six by her mother, who was a black belt herself. Little did she know that this introduction would set her on a path to greatness. Despite the challenges of her upbringing, Kayla found solace and purpose on the judo mats, where she quickly excelled under the guidance of her coach, Daniel Doyle.

However, Kayla's journey was not without its hardships. At a young age, she faced unimaginable trauma when she became a victim of sexual abuse at the hands of her coach. Instead of succumbing to despair, Kayla showed incredible courage by speaking out against her abuser and seeking justice. This experience not only shaped her resilience but also fueled her determination to succeed in the sport she loved.

In the midst of adversity, Kayla's talent shone bright. By the age of 15, she had already won two national championships, showcasing her exceptional skill and dedication to her craft. Despite the challenges she faced off the mat, Kayla remained focused on her goals, determined to carve out a path for herself in the world of judo.

Kayla's breakthrough came when she transitioned to the −78 kg weight class in 2008, a move that would set the stage for her remarkable success on the international stage. In the same year, she won the Junior World Championship, becoming the first American to compete in two Junior World Championships finals—an impressive feat for any athlete.

But it was her performance at the 2012 London Olympics that would catapult Kayla into the spotlight and etch her name into the annals of judo history. Against all odds, she clinched the gold medal in the −78 kg category, making her the first American woman to achieve such a feat. Her victory not only brought glory to her country but also inspired a generation of aspiring judokas around the world.

Building on her Olympic success, Kayla continued to dominate the judo circuit, winning gold medals at the World Championships and Pan American Games. Her unparalleled skill and tenacity made her a force to be reckoned with on the mat, earning her a rightful place among the greatest judokas of all time.

As Kayla's star continued to rise, she faced a new challenge—transitioning to mixed martial arts (MMA). In the face of uncertainty, she embraced this new chapter with characteristic determination, proving herself as a formidable force in the cage.

From her humble beginnings in Middletown to her meteoric rise to the top of the MMA world, Kayla Harrison's journey is a testament to the power of resilience, determination, and unwavering belief in oneself. As she continues to defy expectations and break barriers, her story serves as an inspiration to countless individuals around the globe, reminding us that with hard work and perseverance, anything is possible.

Chapter 1: Early Years and Judo Journey

Kayla Harrison's early years were shaped by the influence of her family and a natural inclination towards athleticism. Born on July 2, 1990, in Middletown, Ohio, Kayla grew up in a supportive environment where she was encouraged to pursue her passions. It was her mother who first introduced her to the world of judo, igniting a lifelong love affair with the sport.

From a young age, Kayla displayed a remarkable aptitude for physical activities. Whether it was playing sports with her siblings or engaging in outdoor adventures, she thrived in environments that challenged her physical prowess. When her mother, a black belt in judo, suggested that she try the sport, Kayla eagerly embraced the opportunity.

Judo quickly became more than just a recreational activity for Kayla—it became a passion and a way of life. Under the guidance of her mother and other judo instructors, she learned the fundamentals of the sport and discovered a sense of purpose on the mats. Judo provided Kayla with a platform to channel her energy, develop discipline, and cultivate important life skills such as perseverance and resilience.

As Kayla immersed herself in judo training, her natural talent became increasingly apparent. She demonstrated an innate understanding of the sport's techniques and strategies, quickly rising through the ranks in local competitions. Her dedication and hard work were evident to all who knew her, and it wasn't long before she began to garner attention on the national stage.

Despite her early success in judo, Kayla's journey was marred by a traumatic experience that threatened to derail her promising career. At the age of 15, she became the victim of sexual abuse at the hands of her coach, Daniel Doyle. This devastating betrayal shattered Kayla's trust and left her grappling with feelings of fear, shame, and confusion.

In the face of such adversity, Kayla demonstrated incredible courage and resilience. She refused to remain silent about the abuse, bravely speaking out against her abuser and seeking justice for herself and others who may have been victimized. Her decision to come forward was met with immense support from her family, friends, and the judo community, who rallied around her in solidarity.

Chapter 2: Olympic Triumphs and World Championships

The pinnacle of any judoka's career is often the Olympic Games, where they have the opportunity to compete on the world's biggest stage and etch their names into the annals of sporting history. For Kayla Harrison, the 2012 and 2016 Olympics were not just opportunities to compete—they were chances to make history and solidify her status as one of the greatest judokas of all time.

At the 2012 London Olympics, Kayla arrived as a relative unknown on the international stage, despite her impressive track record in national and Pan American competitions. Competing in the −78 kg weight category, she faced stiff competition from seasoned veterans and rising stars alike. However, Kayla's determination and skill shone through as she blazed a trail to the top of the podium.

In a series of electrifying matches, Kayla showcased her technical prowess and tactical acumen, dispatching opponents with precision and finesse. Her relentless pursuit of victory and unwavering focus propelled her to the final, where she faced Gemma Gibbons of Britain in a highly anticipated showdown. In a thrilling display of athleticism and determination, Kayla emerged victorious, clinching the gold medal and etching her name into the history books as the first American woman to win an Olympic gold medal in judo.

Four years later, at the 2016 Rio Olympics, Kayla returned to defend her title and cement her status as one of the sport's greatest champions. Despite facing heightened expectations and increased pressure, she rose to the occasion with characteristic poise and determination. Once again competing in the −78 kg weight category, Kayla showcased her dominance on the mat, dispatching opponents with ease and precision.

In the final, she faced off against Audrey Tcheuméo of France, a formidable opponent with whom she shared a storied rivalry. In a tense and hard-fought contest, Kayla once again emerged victorious, securing her second consecutive Olympic gold medal and solidifying her status as one of the sport's all-time greats. Her back-to-back gold medal triumphs were a testament to her skill, determination, and unwavering commitment to excellence, inspiring a new generation of judokas around the world.

In addition to her Olympic triumphs, Kayla Harrison also enjoyed immense success on the world stage, winning gold medals at the World Championships and Pan American Games. These competitions served as opportunities for Kayla to showcase her skills and test herself against the best judokas from around the globe, further solidifying her reputation as a dominant force in the sport.

At the World Championships, Kayla faced off against the best judokas in the world, competing in a grueling series of matches to prove her mettle on the international stage. Despite the intense competition and fierce rivalries, she consistently rose to the occasion, demonstrating her technical proficiency and strategic prowess to emerge victorious time and time again.

Her gold medal triumphs at the World Championships not only showcased her individual talent but also underscored her importance as a key member of the US judo team, inspiring her teammates to strive for greatness and achieve their own personal bests.

Similarly, at the Pan American Games, Kayla continued to dominate the competition, winning gold medals and solidifying her status as the undisputed queen of the −78 kg weight category. Her performances at these prestigious events not only brought glory to her country but also elevated the sport of judo to new heights, inspiring a new generation of athletes to pursue their dreams with passion and determination.

Kayla's success on the world stage was a testament to her talent, dedication, and unwavering commitment to excellence. Her Olympic triumphs and world championship victories will forever be remembered as defining moments in the history of judo, cementing her legacy as one of the sport's all-time greats and inspiring countless individuals around the world to pursue their own dreams with courage and conviction.

Chapter 3: Transition to Mixed Martial Arts

After achieving unprecedented success in judo, including back-to-back Olympic gold medals and numerous world championships, Kayla Harrison faced a pivotal decision: what next? Despite her dominance in the sport of judo, Kayla hungered for new challenges and opportunities to push herself to the limits of her athletic abilities. It was this drive for self-improvement and the allure of a new challenge that ultimately led her to make the transition to mixed martial arts (MMA).

The decision to enter the world of MMA was not one that Kayla took lightly. As a lifelong judoka, she had spent years honing her skills and mastering the intricacies of her craft. However, the prospect of testing herself in a new environment, against opponents with different skill sets and fighting styles was too enticing to resist.

In addition to the allure of competition, Kayla was also drawn to the potential for personal growth and development that MMA offered. Unlike judo, which is primarily a grappling-based sport, MMA is a multidisciplinary discipline that encompasses a wide range of techniques and strategies, including striking, wrestling, and Brazilian jiu-jitsu. For Kayla, the opportunity to learn and master new skills was an exciting prospect—one that promised to challenge her both physically and mentally.

But perhaps the most compelling reason for Kayla's decision to enter MMA was the opportunity to inspire others. Throughout her career, she had served as a role model and mentor to countless aspiring athletes, particularly young girls, who looked up to her as a symbol of strength, resilience, and determination. By stepping into the world of MMA, Kayla hoped to continue this legacy of inspiration, showing others that with hard work, dedication, and perseverance, anything is possible.

Kayla Harrison's transition to MMA was met with much anticipation and excitement from fans and pundits alike. As a two-time

Olympic gold medalist and one of the most decorated judokas in history, she brought with her a wealth of talent, experience, and expertise to the world of professional fighting.

Kayla's early years in MMA were marked by a period of adjustment and learning, as she adapted to the unique demands and challenges of the sport. Gone were the familiar confines of the judo mat, replaced instead by the unforgiving canvas of the MMA cage. It was a steep learning curve, but Kayla approached it with characteristic determination and tenacity, refusing to be daunted by the obstacles that lay ahead.

One of the biggest challenges that Kayla faced in her early MMA career was adapting her judo-centric skill set to the diverse and dynamic nature of mixed martial arts. While her judo background provided her with a solid foundation in grappling and takedown techniques, she soon realized that she needed to expand her repertoire to include striking and ground fighting if she hoped to succeed in the world of MMA.

Under the guidance of her coaches and training partners, Kayla embarked on a rigorous regimen of training and preparation, focusing on improving her striking, wrestling, and Brazilian jiu-jitsu skills. She sparred with seasoned MMA fighters, soaking up knowledge and experience from those who had walked the path before her, and honing her craft with each passing day.

Despite the steep learning curve, Kayla's talent and determination quickly became evident in the cage. In her professional debut at PFL 2 on June 21, 2018, she faced off against Brittney Elkin in the Women's Lightweight division. In a display of dominance and skill, Kayla secured a submission victory via armbar in the first round, announcing her arrival on the MMA scene in emphatic fashion.

From that moment on, Kayla's star continued to rise in the world of MMA. With each successive fight, she showcased her talent and versatility, earning victories over a series of tough opponents and solidifying her status as one of the sport's rising stars. Her early success in MMA was a testament to her talent, work ethic, and unwavering commitment to excellence, setting the stage for what promised to be a truly remarkable career in the cage.

Chapter 4: PFL Domination and Rising Stardom

Kayla Harrison's entry into the Professional Fighters League (PFL) marked the beginning of a new chapter in her MMA career—one characterized by dominance, determination, and a relentless pursuit of excellence. From the moment she stepped into the PFL cage, Kayla proved to be a force to be reckoned with, leaving a trail of destruction in her wake and solidifying her status as one of the most formidable fighters in the promotion.

In her debut season with the PFL in 2018, Kayla wasted no time in making her mark on the organization. Competing in the

Women's Lightweight division, she steamrolled through her opponents with ease, showcasing her superior grappling skills and relentless aggression inside the cage. With each successive fight, Kayla seemed to grow stronger and more confident, dispatching her rivals with a combination of precision strikes and devastating submissions.

By the end of the season, Kayla had firmly established herself as the woman to beat in the Women's Lightweight division, culminating in a championship victory at PFL 10 on December 31, 2019. In a dominant performance, she defeated Larissa Pacheco to claim the 2019 Women's Lightweight Championship, capping off an undefeated season and cementing her status as the top fighter in her weight class.

But Kayla's success in the PFL was far from over. In the following seasons, she continued to dominate the competition, racking up victories and championships with seemingly effortless ease. Her unparalleled skill and athleticism made her a nightmare matchup for any opponent, as she consistently outclassed and outperformed her rivals in every aspect of the game.

In addition to her individual success, Kayla's dominance in the PFL helped to elevate the organization to new heights, drawing attention and acclaim from fans and pundits alike. Her thrilling fights and awe-inspiring performances captivated audiences around the world, bringing new eyes to the sport of MMA and solidifying the PFL as a premier destination for top-tier talent.

As Kayla Harrison's star continued to rise in the world of MMA, she quickly emerged as a household name and one of the sport's most recognizable figures. Her dominance in the cage and her compelling back-story—highlighted by her Olympic success and her courageous stance against sexual abuse—captured the imagination of fans and media alike, propelling her to new heights of fame and popularity.

Kayla's impact on the MMA scene extended far beyond her performances inside the cage. As a two-time Olympic gold medalist and one of the most decorated judokas in history, she brought a level of skill, athleticism, and professionalism to the sport that was unmatched by her peers. Her technical prowess and strategic acumen made her a role model for aspiring fighters around the world, inspiring a new generation of athletes to pursue their dreams with passion and determination.

But perhaps even more impressive than her success in the cage was Kayla's commitment to using her platform for positive change. Throughout her career, she has been a vocal advocate for survivors of sexual abuse, using her own experiences as a catalyst for change and empowerment. Through her work with organizations such as the #MeToo movement and the SafeSport initiative,

Kayla has sought to raise awareness about the prevalence of sexual abuse in sports and to empower survivors to speak out and seek justice.

In addition to her advocacy work, Kayla has also become a sought-after commentator and analyst, providing expert insight and analysis on MMA events and matchups. Her articulate commentary and engaging personality have endeared her to fans and pundits alike, further solidifying her status as a respected figure in the MMA community.

As Kayla Harrison's star continues to rise, there is no doubt that she will remain a dominant force in the world of MMA for years to come. Her remarkable talent, unwavering determination, and commitment to excellence have made her a true trailblazer in the sport, and her impact on the MMA scene will be felt for generations to come.

Chapter 5: Signing with Bellator MMA and Return to PFL

Kayla Harrison's decision to sign with Bellator MMA marked a significant turning point in her career, as she embarked on a new chapter in the world of mixed martial arts. The move to Bellator represented an opportunity for Kayla to test herself against a new roster of competitors and further solidify her status as one of the sport's premier athletes. However, her decision to sign with Bellator was not without controversy, as it sparked a contract dispute with her former promotion, the Professional Fighters League (PFL).

The signing with Bellator was met with much excitement and anticipation from fans and pundits alike, who eagerly awaited Kayla's debut in the promotion. As a two-time Olympic gold medalist and reigning PFL champion, Kayla brought with her a level of talent and prestige that few fighters could match, making her a prized acquisition for Bellator.

However, the announcement of Kayla's signing with Bellator also reignited a longstanding contract dispute with the PFL, who claimed that they had exercised their matching rights to retain Kayla's services for another season. The dispute quickly escalated into a legal battle, with both sides digging in their heels and refusing to back down.

For Kayla, the contract controversy was a frustrating distraction from her training and preparation for her upcoming fights. As the legal proceedings dragged on, she found herself caught in the middle of a bitter dispute between two rival promotions, unsure of when—or if—she would be able to return to the cage.

Despite the contract controversy swirling around her, Kayla remained focused on her ultimate goal: reclaiming her status as the top fighter in the Women's Lightweight division. After months of uncertainty and legal wrangling, Kayla finally received the news she had been waiting for: she was cleared to return to the PFL and defend her championship title.

The announcement of Kayla's return to the PFL was met with much excitement and anticipation from fans and pundits alike, who eagerly awaited her comeback to the cage. For Kayla, it was a chance to put the contract controversy behind her and focus on what she did best: winning fights and dominating her opponents.

In her return to the PFL, Kayla wasted no time in picking up where she left off, dispatching opponents with ease and precision. With each successive victory, she silenced her critics and reaffirmed her status as one of the most dominant fighters in the promotion, proving once again that she was a force to be reckoned with inside the cage.

But perhaps even more impressive than her victories inside the cage was Kayla's resilience and determination in the face of adversity. Despite the challenges and setbacks she faced, she never wavered in her commitment to her craft, continuing to train and prepare with the same intensity and focus that had made her a champion in the first place.

As Kayla's star continues to rise in the world of MMA, there is no doubt that she will remain a dominant force in the sport for years to come. Her remarkable talent, unwavering determination, and commitment to excellence have made her a true trailblazer in the world of mixed martial arts, and her impact on the sport will be felt for generations to come.

Chapter 6: UFC Debut and Beyond

Kayla Harrison's journey to the Ultimate Fighting Championship (UFC) was a culmination of years of hard work, dedication, and relentless pursuit of excellence. As one of the most decorated judokas in history and a dominant force in the world of mixed martial arts (MMA), Kayla had long set her sights on competing in the UFC—the pinnacle of the sport.

The announcement of Kayla's signing with the UFC sent shockwaves through the MMA world, as fans and pundits alike eagerly awaited her debut on the sport's biggest stage. For Kayla, the opportunity to compete in the UFC was a dream come true, representing the culmination of years of sacrifice and determination.

Signing with the UFC not only offered Kayla the opportunity to test herself against the best fighters in the world but also provided her with a platform to showcase her skills and athleticism to a global audience. As one of the UFC's newest signings, Kayla quickly became the center of attention, with fans and media alike eagerly anticipating her debut inside the Octagon.

For Kayla, the opportunity to compete in the UFC was the realization of a lifelong dream—one that she had worked tirelessly to achieve. As she prepared to step into the Octagon for the first time, she knew that the eyes of the world would be upon her, watching as she embarked on the next chapter of her storied career.

On April 13, 2024, Kayla Harrison made her much-anticipated UFC debut at UFC 300, facing off against former UFC Women's Bantamweight Champion Holly Holm in the co-main event of the evening. The matchup was highly anticipated, pitting two of the most accomplished female fighters in the sport against each other in a battle for supremacy.

From the opening bell, it was clear that Kayla was determined to make a statement in her UFC debut. With her trademark aggression and relentless pressure, she immediately took the fight to Holm, pushing forward with a relentless onslaught of strikes and takedowns.

Despite Holm's best efforts to counter Kayla's relentless attack, she struggled to find her rhythm and was unable to mount any significant offense of her own. Kayla's superior grappling skills and ground control proved to be the difference-maker, as she repeatedly took Holm down to the canvas and unleashed a barrage of strikes from the top position.

As the fight wore on, it became increasingly clear that Kayla was in complete control, dictating the pace and dictating the terms of the engagement. In the second round, she capitalized on a momentary lapse in Holm's defense, seizing her back and locking in a rear-naked choke submission that forced Holm to tap out.

With her victory over Holly Holm, Kayla Harrison made history, becoming the first woman to win an Olympic gold medal in judo and then transition to become a UFC fighter. Her dominant performance inside the Octagon sent shockwaves through the MMA world, establishing her as a legitimate contender in the UFC Women's Bantamweight division and setting the stage for what promised to be a truly remarkable career in the promotion.

But for Kayla, the victory over Holm was about more than just making history—it was about proving to herself and the world that she belonged among the elite fighters in the

UFC. As she celebrated her victory inside the Octagon, she knew that her journey was just beginning, and that the best was yet to come.

Conclusion

As we reflect on the remarkable career of Kayla Harrison, one thing becomes abundantly clear: her impact on the world of sports transcends mere accolades and achievements. Throughout her journey, Kayla has not only established herself as one of the most dominant athletes in her respective disciplines but has also emerged as a symbol of inspiration, resilience, and empowerment for countless individuals around the world.

From her early days as a judo prodigy to her meteoric rise in the world of mixed martial arts, Kayla's journey is a testament to the power of perseverance, determination, and unwavering belief in oneself. Despite facing numerous challenges and setbacks along the way, she never wavered in her commitment to her craft, continually pushing herself to new heights of excellence and inspiring others to do the same.

But perhaps even more impressive than her athletic achievements is Kayla's unwavering commitment to using her platform for positive change. Throughout her career, she has been a vocal advocate for survivors of sexual abuse, using her own experiences as a catalyst for change and empowerment. Through her work with organizations such as the #MeToo movement and the SafeSport initiative, Kayla has sought to raise awareness about the prevalence of sexual abuse in sports and to empower survivors to speak out and seek justice.

In addition to her advocacy work, Kayla has also become a role model and mentor to countless aspiring athletes, particularly young girls, who look up to her as a symbol of strength, resilience, and determination. By sharing her story and leading by example, she has inspired a new generation of athletes to pursue their dreams with passion and determination, showing them that with hard work, dedication, and perseverance, anything is possible.

As Kayla Harrison looks to the future, the possibilities are endless. With her unparalleled talent, unwavering determination, and commitment to excellence, there is no doubt that she will continue to leave an indelible mark on the world of mixed martial arts for years to come.

In the short term, Kayla's focus will undoubtedly be on further establishing herself as a dominant force in the UFC Women's Bantamweight division. With her victory over Holly Holm at UFC 300, she has already proven that she belongs among the elite fighters in the promotion, and she will undoubtedly be looking to build on that success in the months and years ahead.

But beyond her immediate goals in the UFC, Kayla's impact on the sport extends far beyond the confines of the Octagon. As a trailblazer and role model, she has paved the way for future generations of athletes to follow in her footsteps, showing them that with hard work, dedication, and perseverance, anything is possible.

In the years to come, we can expect to see Kayla continue to inspire and empower others through her advocacy work, mentorship, and leadership both inside and outside the cage. Whether she's fighting for championships in the UFC or fighting for justice and equality outside of it, one thing is for certain: Kayla Harrison's legacy will endure for generations to come, leaving an indelible mark on the world of sports and inspiring countless individuals to reach for the stars.

Made in the USA
Las Vegas, NV
28 May 2024